Pincushion Appeal

Patterns for Pincushions to Make You Smile

Cecile McPeak and Rachel Martin

Martingale®
Create with Confidence

Pincushion Appeal:
Patterns for Pincushions to Make You Smile
© 2013 by Cecile McPeak and Rachel Martin

Martingale®
19021 120th Ave. NE, Ste. 102
Bothell, WA 98011-9511 USA
ShopMartingale.com

Printed in China
18 17 16 15 14 13   8 7 6 5 4 3 2 1

Library of Congress Cataloging-in-Publication Data is available upon request.

ISBN: 978-1-60468-361-5

Mission Statement

Dedicated to providing quality products and service to inspire creativity.

Credits

PRESIDENT AND CEO: Tom Wierzbicki

EDITOR IN CHIEF: Mary V. Green

DESIGN DIRECTOR: Paula Schlosser

MANAGING EDITOR: Karen Costello Soltys

ACQUISITIONS EDITOR: Karen M. Burns

TECHNICAL EDITOR: Laurie Baker

COPY EDITOR: Sheila Chapman Ryan

PRODUCTION MANAGER: Regina Girard

COVER AND INTERIOR DESIGNER: Connor Chin

PHOTOGRAPHER: Brent Kane

ILLUSTRATOR: Christine Erikson

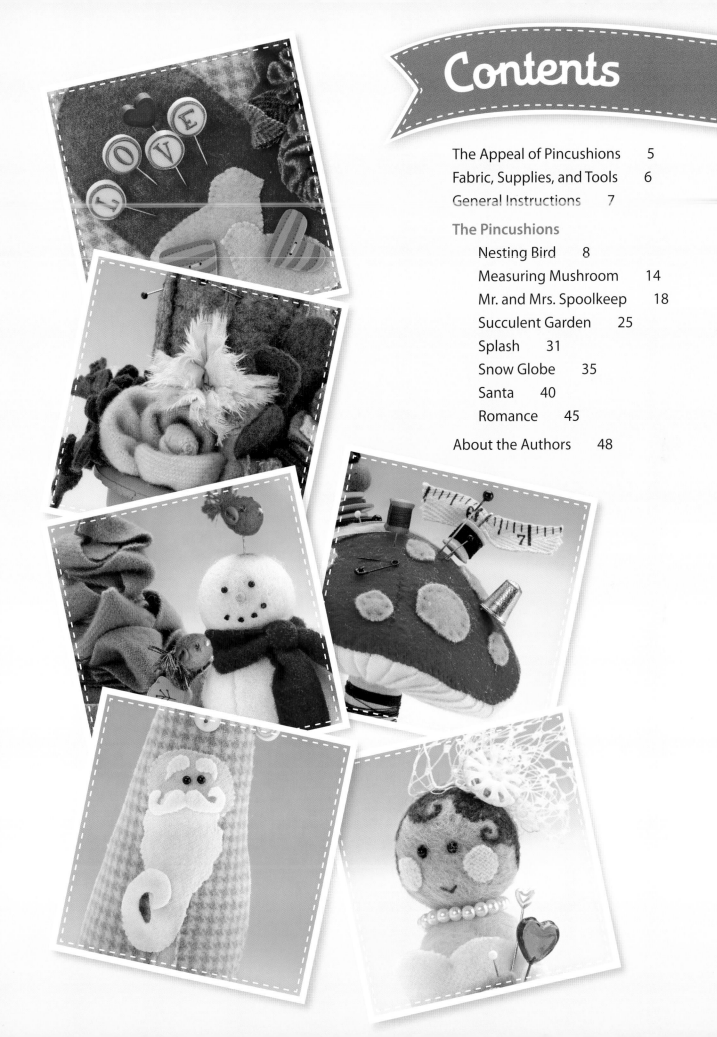

Contents

The Appeal of Pincushions   5

Fabric, Supplies, and Tools   6

General Instructions   7

The Pincushions

    Nesting Bird   8

    Measuring Mushroom   14

    Mr. and Mrs. Spoolkeep   18

    Succulent Garden   25

    Splash   31

    Snow Globe   35

    Santa   40

    Romance   45

About the Authors   48

The Appeal of Pincushions

Pins have served many uses since prehistoric man first used sharp thorns as fasteners. Long before buttons and zippers were mass-produced, pins made from bone, horn, wood, and eventually metal were prized for decorative and useful purposes. By the Middle Ages, a portion of a household budget was commonly set aside as "pin money" to ensure an adequate supply of metal pins. Pins continued to be handmade by skilled craftsmen until the early 1800s, so they remained expensive and in limited supply.

Pincushions evolved as a means of storing and preserving these valued items. Thrifty women made practical pincushions from scraps of fabric. Well-to-do women of the eighteenth and nineteenth centuries kept pins on their dressing tables in ornate pincushions. Whether the pins were used for sewing or for dressing, these pincushions served a practical purpose. Now we likely see pincushions as ephemera rather than household necessities. But for many of us, pincushions have another purpose. They are expressions of creativity—small bits of art.

On the following pages, you'll find eight pincushions to make. We'll start by covering the best fabrics to use, the tools and supplies you'll need for creating your pincushion, and the basic techniques used throughout the book. These pincushions can be accomplished by a beginner, and some can be assembled in as little as twenty minutes with a needle and thread or a bit of glue. Because of the small size, the expense is minimal. Despite the simplicity of construction, the end result is a handmade work of art as well as a functional pincushion. Visit our website (www.ThePincushionEffect.com) to see how we display these pincushions.

Are you ready to create some pincushion appeal of your own? We think you are!

–Cecile and Rachel

Fabric, Supplies, and Tools

You'll find that most of the items you need to create your own pincushion appeal are already on your sewing or craft shelf, and if they're not, we've included information for suppliers of many of these products in "Resources" (page 48). The following list gives you an idea of the items you'll want to have on hand—and remember, hunting is half the fun!

Felted wool. Many of the pincushions in this book are made using felted wool from Weeks Dye Works. This high-quality, woven wool is hand dyed and available in lots of colors and patterns. Felted wool is especially wonderful because it doesn't unravel. Try leaving the seam allowances on the outside for extra texture.

While felted wool is fiarly expensive, none of it goes to waste. Small pieces can be cut into flowers, leaves, and other embellishments. It's also a beginner-friendly fabric. It has a little natural stretch, so curved pieces go together easily, and the sturdy weight means that uneven stitching and stuffing is easily disguised.

Wool-blend felt. A nonwoven, wool-rayon blend (such as WoolFelt from National Nonwovens), wool-blend felt is available from craft and fabric stores. It has a thin, flat profile so it's good for projects like "Mr. and Mrs. Spool-keep" (page 18). To give larger pieces of wool-blend felt interesting texture, machine wash and tumble dry before cutting. We did this for the mushroom cap in "Measuring Mushroom" (page 14) and the cactus in "Succulent Garden" (page 25).

Wool roving. Roving is a bundle of cleaned and carded fibers ready to be spun into yarn or flattened and used as batting. It's ideal for stuffing pincushions because pins go into it easily. Polyester stuffing is less expensive than wool and can be substituted for roving.

Crushed walnut shells. You can add weight to your pincushion by partially filling it with crushed walnut shells before completely stuffing it with roving or polyester stuffing. You can find crushed walnut shells in most pet stores.

Felted-wool balls. These 100% wool balls are available from HandBEHG Felts in several sizes and can be rolled to reshape. They can be sewn or glued to other materials or used as pincushions all by themselves. Sew a flat button to the bottom of a ball to make it stand by itself.

Decorative pins. Purchase decorative pins or make some using a variety of beads and found objects. Glue the embellishments to new or old pins in a variety of lengths. Just Another Button Company sells the handmade polymer-clay pins shown on some of our pincushions (see "Resources").

Beads, buttons, and trims. Look through your stash for new and vintage items to embellish your pincushions with interesting details. Small beads or buttons can be used for texture or eyes.

Floral wire. Enclose silver 20-gauge floral wire between layers of wool to make poseable pincushion features.

Embroidery floss. Hand embroider details with the number of strands of floss indicated in the project instructions.

Cardboard. Sometimes a pincushion needs a little structure. Cardboard is a good choice because it's always handy. A cereal box will work when lightweight cardboard is called for; mat-board scraps work best when heavyweight cardboard is needed.

Wooden spools. Hot glue a pincushion to a wooden spool for display. We've used spools of all sizes, including large ones from textile mills, for this purpose. If the spool still has thread wound around it, you can secure the thread by gluing a tiny button over the thread end.

Basic tools and supplies. You'll need the following items for assembling the projects in this book:

- » Freezer paper
- » Sharp pencil
- » Scissors for fabric and paper
- » Iron and ironing surface
- » Tailor's chalk
- » Yardstick or long quilter's ruler
- » Straight pins
- » Hand-sewing needles in various sizes, including size 24 chenille needles for embroidery and size 10 Sharps for general sewing
- » All-purpose thread in assorted colors
- » Hot-glue gun and glue sticks
- » Superglue
- » Fine-tip permanent markers in brown, black, and orange
- » Wire cutters
- » Needle-nose pliers
- » Scotch tape

The techniques used to make the pincushions in this book aren't difficult, but you'll need to know a few basics.

Making the Patterns

With a pencil, trace each of the patterns for your project onto the dull side of a piece of freezer paper. Trace all the markings from the pattern in the book onto the freezer-paper patterns; also transfer any labels indicating wool type and color or stitching instructions. Roughly cut out each pattern.

Cutting Out and Marking the Fabric Pieces

Place each pattern, shiny side down, onto the fabric indicated. With a dry iron on the wool setting, press the pattern in place; let it cool, and then cut out the piece on the marked outer line. With the freezer-paper pattern still in place, poke a dull pencil through the freezer paper *only* at each dot on the pattern. On dark fabric, twirl the pencil to make a slightly larger hole in the pattern, and then rub over the hole with tailor's chalk to mark the dot on the fabric. On light fabric, press the pencil through the hole and lightly mark the dot on the fabric. Remove the freezer paper and take a few small stitches at each mark. Remove these stitches when you've completed your pincushion.

Note: For darts, you only need to mark the dots at the beginning and end of the dart on the fabric. The center fold line and outer stitching lines are for reference only.

Sewing

Hand or machine sew all seams using a 1/8" seam allowance unless otherwise indicated. Stitch darts by first folding the piece on the dart fold line, and then stitching the dart from the dot marked at the point to the edge of the piece. Finger-press the dart flat.

Making a Pincushion Base

Cut a circle of wool or fabric that's 1" larger than the mat-board or cardboard base. Gather the fabric around the base with a running stitch. Tuck a circle of cardboard the same size as your base inside the bottom of the pincushion and gather the bottom edge of the pincushion around the cardboard. With the gathered sides facing each other, place the covered base circle against the circle inside the pincushion. Hand sew the pieces together around the circles.

Hand Stitching

Many of the projects require hand stitching, either for function or as a decorative element. Use thread or embroidery floss as indicated in the project instructions to make your stitches. If you're using thread, a size chenille 10 Sharp needle will work for most tasks; use a size 24 needle when working with embroidery floss.

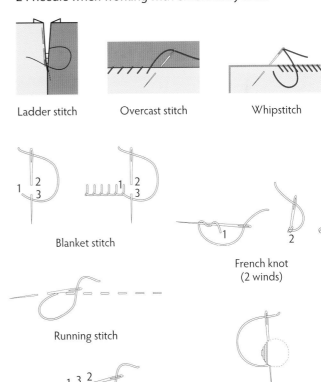

Ladder stitch   Overcast stitch   Whipstitch

Blanket stitch

French knot (2 winds)

Running stitch

Satin stitch

Stem stitch

*T*he edges of felted wool don't fray, so the wing and tail feathers of this adorable bird have dimensional interest without seams—perfect for a hand-sewn project. Add vintage appeal with old hat pins and a large wooden spool, and use the N-is-for-Nest pin set from Just Another Button Company for a touch of whimsy.

Finished size: 6" x 6" x 3¾" (bird only)
6" x 9" x 3¾" (bird with top embellishment)
6" x 19" x 4" (bird on spool)

Materials

12" x 12" square of teal houndstooth felted wool for bird

6" x 9" piece of dark-brown felted wool for tail and wings

3" length of ⅝"-wide gold velvet ribbon for beak

2 black ¼"-diameter beads for eyes

4 yards of ⅜"-wide dark-brown solid grosgrain ribbon for nest

1 yard *each* of assorted brown, teal, and aqua grosgrain ribbons, ⅜", ⅝", and ⅞" wide, for nest (6 yards total; we used solid, polka-dot, and edge-stitched ribbons)

15 assorted ½"- to 1"-diameter mother-of-pearl buttons for nest and bird

Metal or plastic ring, 5" diameter, *OR* 5"-diameter plastic lid for nest base

4 silver 20-gauge floral stem wires, 18" long

10" x 10" square of water-soluble stabilizer (such as Solvy)

6-strand embroidery floss: dark brown

Wool roving or polyester stuffing

Vintage wooden spool, 10" tall

Basic tools and supplies (page 6)

Optional embellishments: Nest pins (from Just Another Button Company; see "Resources" on page 48)

Cutting

From *each* of the teal and dark-brown felted wools, cut:
1 rectangle, 3½" x 5"

Make the Ribbon Nest

1 If you're using a plastic lid for the base of the nest, place the lid on a cutting board and use a craft knife to cut an X in the center. Insert your scissor blades through the X and cut out the center of the lid, leaving the rim intact. Discard the center of the lid.

2 Cut the dark-brown and assorted ⅜"-wide ribbons into 6½"-long pieces and the assorted ⅝"- and ⅞"-wide ribbons into 8½"-long pieces.

3 Lay out the ribbon pieces side by side on your workspace in the order you'll tie them to the ring or lid base. Begin with the longer ribbon strips, alternating the patterns and colors as you lay them out. Add a strip of one of the narrower ribbons between each of the longer pieces, again alternating the colors.

4 Working in order, tie the ribbons to the base. Tie the ⅞"- and ⅝"-wide ribbons to the base with a lark's head knot and the ⅜"-wide ribbons with an overhand knot (page 10). Secure each lark's head knot with a few tacking stitches worked from the side to hide the stitches.

The narrow ribbons will stay knotted if you pull them tightly. Push the ribbons close together as you finish each one.

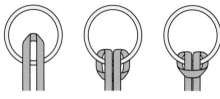

Lark's head knot

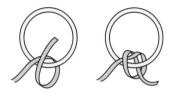

Overhand knot

5 Set aside one of the larger mother-of-pearl buttons for the bird's tail, and then select seven assorted mother-of-pearl buttons and randomly stitch them to the knots, referring to the photo (page 8) for placement ideas.

6 Cut each of the floral wires in half with wire cutters. Bend a small hook at the end of one wire. Thread the unbent end of the wire through the hole of a button from the front to the back. Slide the button to the hooked end of the wire so the hook goes through the second hole of the button. With needle-nose pliers, bend the hook across the back of the button to hold it in place. Then wrap the long end of the wire around a pencil to coil it and slide the pencil out. Repeat to make eight embellished wires.

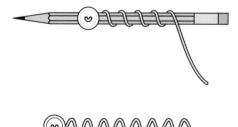

7 Twist the free end of an embellished wire around the circle base of the nest between two ribbon knots. Add the remaining wires in the same way. Bend and arrange the coiled wires in interesting positions and fluff the ribbon knots, referring to the photo as needed.

Make the Wing and Tail Pieces

1 Use the patterns (pages 12 and 13) and refer to "General Instructions" (page 7) to make templates and cut out the pieces from the fabrics indicated. Mark the dots.

2 Trace the right and left wing shapes onto the stabilizer; include the embroidery lines. Roughly cut out the shapes. Pin the stabilizer pieces to the appropriate wool wing piece, lining up the outer lines of the traced shapes with the edge of the fabric pieces.

3 Using three strands of dark-brown floss, stem stitch (page 7) along the traced inner lines of each wing, stitching through both layers. When the embroidery is complete, remove the stabilizer following the manufacturer's instructions. Allow the wings to air dry; do not apply heat.

4 Pin the embroidered wings onto the remainder of the dark-brown wool, allowing ¼" of the dark-brown wool to show around each wing. With a single strand of matching thread, hand sew a small running stitch through both wool layers ⅛" inside the cut edges of the teal wool. Cut around the wings, leaving ⅛" of brown wool showing around each pieces.

5 Sandwich the dark-brown wool rectangle between the tail piece and the teal wool rectangle. With matching thread and the sharp needle, hand sew a small running stitch ⅛" from the tail piece edge to join all three wool layers. Also, stitch the feather detail lines, referring to the pattern as needed. If needed, mark the lines on a piece of stabilizer and stitch through it as you did for the wing embroidery.

6 Cut around the tail piece, cutting through the brown and teal rectangles and leaving ⅛" of brown wool showing around the tail. Turn over the tail to the back and, holding the scissors flat against the teal wool, trim away most of the teal wool outside the stitching line so the brown wool shows around the outside edges.

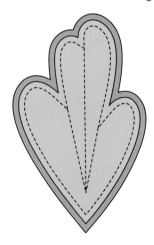

Assemble the Body

1 Match the dots on each end of the gusset piece to the dots on either the left or right body piece, working across the bottom of the body. Pin the pieces together at the dots first, and then pin along the bottom edge, easing the fabric along the curve. Hand or machine sew the gusset in place along the pinned edge, beginning and ending at the marked dots. If hand sewing, use a double strand of matching thread and small stitches.

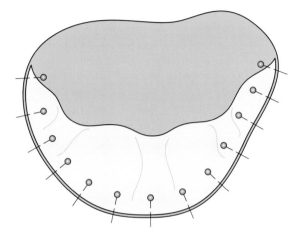

2 Pin the remaining body piece to the remaining side of the gusset, again matching the marked dots and cut edges. Sew the seam between the dots, leaving an opening as indicated on the gusset pattern to turn the body after sewing.

3 Pin the body pieces together along the top edges. Sew the pieces together between the marked dots.

4 Turn the body right side out through the opening in the gusset seam. Stuff firmly with wool roving or polyester stuffing, filling the head and front of the body first. Tuck the seam allowance of the opening to the inside and sew the opening closed.

5 Tack the wings to the body, referring to the pattern pieces for placement. Tack the tail to the back of the

body and sew a button at the base of the tail over the gusset point.

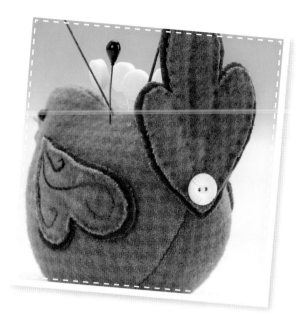

6 Using a size 10 Sharp needle and black thread, take a couple of stitches at the point marked for the eye. Place a bead on the needle and stitch through the head, with the needle coming out at the point for the second eye. Place a second bead on the needle and stitch back through the head. Pass through the first bead again and then back through to the second bead, pulling the thread snugly so the eyes indent into the head a little. Secure the thread.

7 Fold the velvet ribbon strip in half, right sides together and matching the cut ends. Hand or machine stitch across the cut ends using a ¼" seam allowance. Clip the corners of the seamed end. Whip-stitch the two layers together along one long edge. Turn the beak right side out.

8 Turn the ribbon so the whipstitched edge is vertical and facing you. Bring the points together so that the seam folds in on itself and the open edges are aligned and form points at the ends. Pin the beak to the body

over the gusset point and tack it in place at the sides and the center top and bottom.

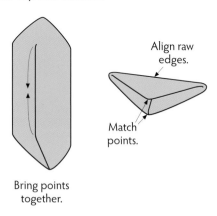

Align raw edges.

Match points.

Bring points together.

Finish and Embellish

1 Using a hot-glue gun, glue the ribbon nest to the end of the wooden spool. Glue the bird inside the nest.

2 Embellish with the nest pin set on the top of the bird.

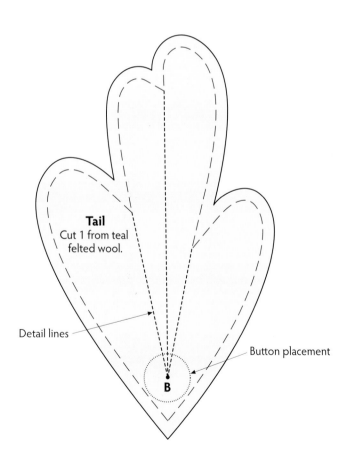

Tail
Cut 1 from teal felted wool.

Detail lines

Button placement

B

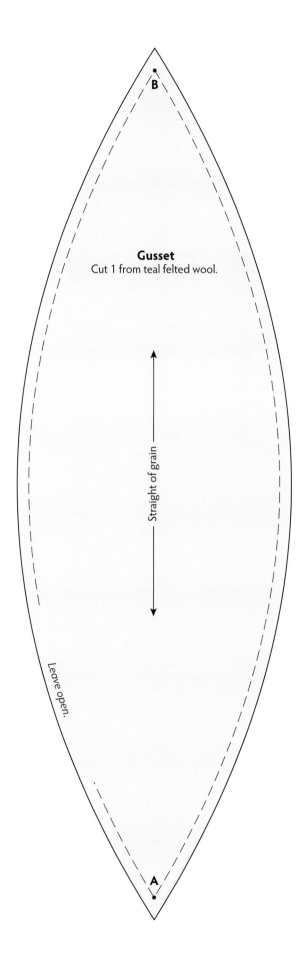

B

Gusset
Cut 1 from teal felted wool.

Straight of grain

Leave open.

A

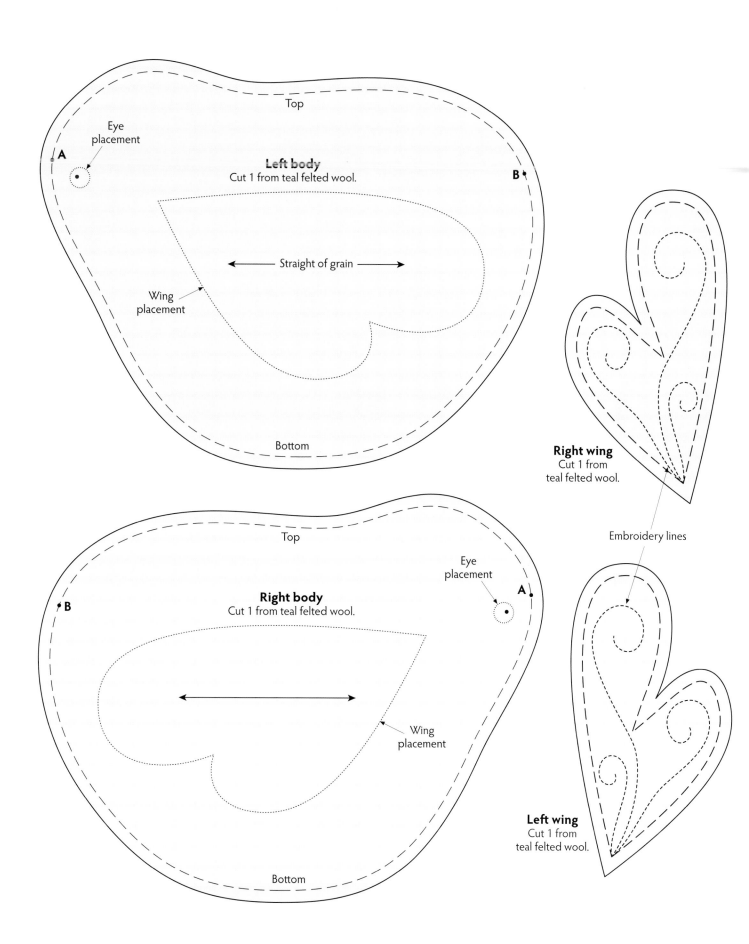

Top

Eye placement

A

Left body
Cut 1 from teal felted wool.

B

Wing placement

Straight of grain

Bottom

Right wing
Cut 1 from
teal felted wool.

Embroidery lines

Top

B

Right body
Cut 1 from teal felted wool.

Eye placement

A

Wing placement

Bottom

Left wing
Cut 1 from
teal felted wool.

*W*ool-blend felt is a good choice for creating the smooth domed shape of the mushroom cap. Use a wooden spool for a stem or scout your sewing room for other options—perhaps a jar of buttons or a ball of pearl cotton.

Finished size: 5" x 5" x 4" (including spool)

Materials

5¼" x 5¼" square of red wool-blend felt for cap

2" x 16" piece of white felted wool for gills

3" x 3" square of lime-green felted wool for cap spots

2"-tall antique wooden spool for stem

Twill tape with ruler motif, 2½" piece

5" x 5" square of mat board

Wool roving or polyester stuffing

5 to 6 assorted 2-hole buttons

1 wooden spool, ½" tall

Darning needle

Corsage pin

1 black bead, 8 mm

Olive felted-wool ball, 1 cm diameter

Assorted sewing charms, buttons, and pins

Basic tools and supplies (page 6)

Optional embellishments: Cranberry ladybug button and avocado spool pin (from Just Another Button Company; see "Resources" on page 48)

Cutting

From the white felted wool, cut:

5 strips, ⅜" x 16"

Make the Mushroom Cap

1 Use the patterns (page 17) and refer to "General Instructions" (page 7) to make the mushroom cap and spot templates and cut out the pieces from the fabrics indicated. Mark the darts.

2 Fold the mushroom cap, right sides together, along the center line of one of the darts. Stitch from the dot at one end to the dot at the other end, referring to the pattern to gently curve the stitching line; secure the thread at each end. Finger-press the fold of fabric flat. Repeat to stitch all of the remaining darts on the mushroom cap.

3 Arrange the lime-green spots on the right side of the mushroom cap where indicated on the pattern or as desired. Hand stitch each spot in place with a single strand of matching thread and a tiny running stitch (page 7) near the edge of the spot, catching the red wool to join the layers.

Make the Mushroom Gills

1 Trace the gill base pattern (page 17) onto mat board and cut it out along the outer line. Cut out the inner circle to make a ring. Carefully bend the mat board up in several places and down in several places to give it a warped appearance.

2 Tape one end of a white wool strip to the wrong side of the mat-board ring. Wrap the strip around the outside of the ring and through the middle, overlapping the edges less at the outer edge and more at the inner edge. Adjust the wraps as necessary to keep the edges of the strip evenly radiating out from the center. The wool at the center will be several layers thick, but that adds extra dimension to the underside of the mushroom. End the strip on the wrong side of the mat board. Thread tack the end to the last full wrap. Start a new strip at the same place, tacking the end to the end of the previous strip. Continue wrapping until the entire mat-board ring is covered.

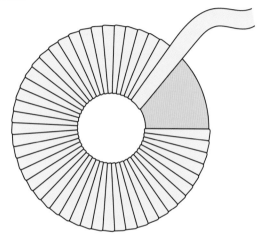

3 Use the tip of your scissors to tuck the edge of the last wrap under the first wrap for a nice finish.

Assemble the Mushroom

1 Lay the mushroom cap on the wrapped ring, wrong sides together. Align the outer edges and pin them in place. With a single strand of red thread, hand stitch the edges together with an overcast stitch (page 7).

2 Fluff the wool roving or polyester stuffing and insert a little at a time through the opening on the underside of the mushroom. Push the stuffing into the edges of the mushroom first, continuing to add more until the pincushion is completely full and firm.

3 Using a hot-glue gun, glue the mushroom top to the top of the wooden spool at a slight angle. Hold the top in place until the glue cools.

Embellish

1 Stitch the ladybug button to a spot on the mushroom cap. Insert the spool pin where desired, referring to the photo if necessary.

2 Thread the twill tape through the eye of the darning needle. Wrap thread around the ½" wooden spool, and then push the spool onto the darning needle up to the twill tape; apply a dab of glue between the pieces to hold them in place.

3 Insert the corsage pin through the black bead, followed by the felted-wool ball. Hold a stack of assorted buttons on the mushroom cap and use the embellished pin to hold them in place.

4 Embellish with additional assorted sewing charms, buttons, and pins as desired.

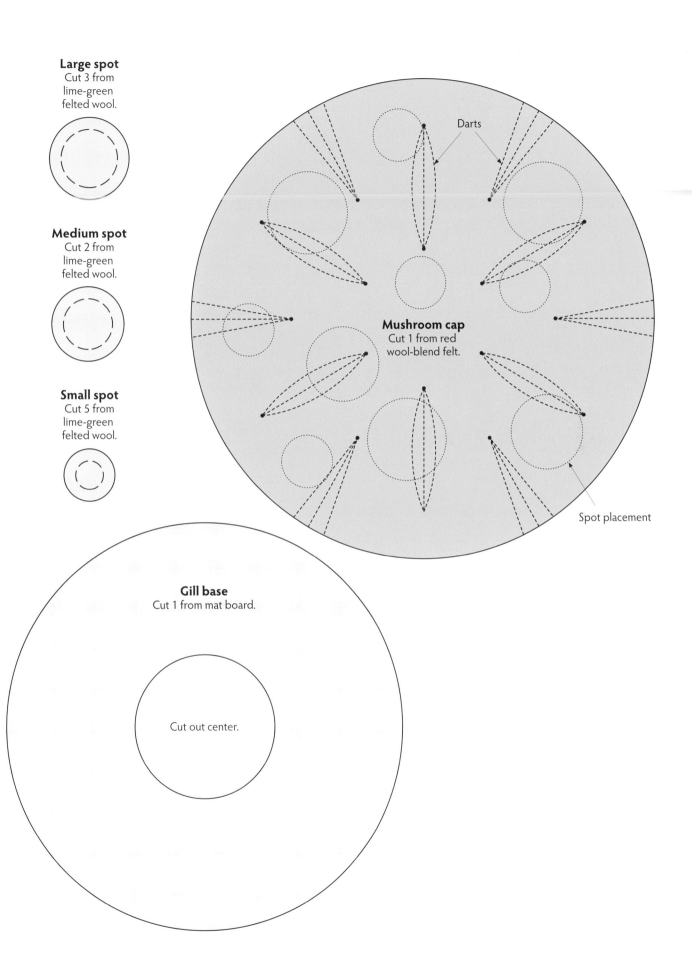

Large spot
Cut 3 from lime-green felted wool.

Medium spot
Cut 2 from lime-green felted wool.

Small spot
Cut 5 from lime-green felted wool.

Darts

Mushroom cap
Cut 1 from red wool-blend felt.

Spot placement

Gill base
Cut 1 from mat board.

Cut out center.

*F*elted-wool balls are functional pincushions on their own and even better when made into spoolkeeps (mini pincushions perched on top of a spool). Add personality to a felted-wool spoolkeep with tiny wool costumes and buttons.

Finished sizes: Mr. Spoolkeep: 2" x 6" x 2"
                        Mrs. Spoolkeep: 4" x 6" x 4"

Materials

3½" x 12" piece of white felted wool for dress and shirt collar

4" x 5" piece of black felted wool for jacket and bow tie

2" x 4" piece of gray glen plaid felted wool for vest

5" x 5½" piece of black wool-blend felt for hat

1½" x 1½" square of green wool-blend felt for bouquet

1½" x 1½" square of light-green felted wool for bouquet

1" x 1" square of pink felted wool for cheeks

2 vintage wooden spools, 2½" tall, wrapped with black thread for Mr. and white thread for Mrs.

2 white and 2 pink felted-wool balls, 3 cm diameter

3" x 9" piece of white netting

6 black seed beads

4 white pearl seed beads

20 pearl beads, 3 mm

6-strand embroidery floss: red

6" length of sheer white ribbon, ⅜" wide

White vintage button, ½" diameter

Flower shank button, ½" diameter

2 flat flower buttons, ½" diameter

2" x 4" piece of mat board

1½" x 15" piece of light weight cardboard

Wool roving or polyester stuffing

Basic tools and supplies (page 6)

Cut the Pieces

1 Use the patterns (pages 23 and 24) and refer to "General Instructions" (page 7) to make the clothing patterns for Mr. and Mrs. Spoolkeep and the cheek pattern for Mrs. Spoolkeep; cut out the pieces from the fabrics indicated. Mark the dart dots on the wrong side of Mrs. Spoolkeep's bodice.

2 Trace the hat-base circle patterns onto mat board and cut them out along the outer line. Cut out the inner circle on each piece to make a ring.

3 Trace the face and hair patterns onto freezer paper and cut them out; set the patterns aside.

Prepare the Spoolkeep Forms

1 Sew a pink felted-wool ball to each white felted-wool ball.

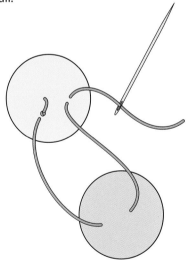

2 Using a hot-glue gun, glue the white felted-wool ball of each stitched pair from step 1 to the top of each wooden spool to create the head and bodies of each pincushion.

3 Lay the traced face and hair patterns on a padded surface. Use a sharp pencil to poke small holes in several places along the hairlines of the hair patterns and at the dots on the face patterns.

4 Pin each face pattern to the center front of the appropriate head. Make a light pencil mark on the head through each pattern hole. Remove the patterns.

5 Using the pencil marks as guides, sew seed beads to each head for the eyes and embroider the mouths with two strands of red floss and a straight stitch. Sew the pink wool cheeks to the Mrs. head with tiny overcast stitches (page 7) and matching thread.

6 Pin the hair patterns to the heads about ¼" from the eyes on the top and sides, aligning the centering lines with the center of the mouths. Make a light pencil mark on each head through the pattern holes. Remove the patterns and connect the dots to draw the hair outlines. The felted-wool balls vary in size, so the patterns may overlap or gap in the back. If that happens, connect the last dots with a straight line.

7 Draw over the pencil hair lines with a black permanent marker for the Mr. and a brown marker for the Mrs. Fill in the hair with the side of the markers, coloring slowly for the best coverage. Allow the ink to dry; then trim off any wool fibers that pulled loose. If pink wool still shows, push the tip of the marker into the wool and twist to fill the area with color.

Make Mr. Spoolkeep

1 Pin the long, unnotched edge of the jacket collar/lapels to the jacket upper edge, matching the A and B dots. Hand sew the pieces together with an overcast stitch and matching thread.

2 Using a hot-glue gun, glue the bow-tie ends together. Wrap the bow-tie strip around the center of the bow and glue the ends of the strip together in the back.

3 Pin the vest pieces together along the overlap line. Sew two black seed beads through both layers at the button-placement marks.

4 Center and pin the shirt collar to the front of the pincushion between the face and body ball. Glue the ends of the collar in place between the balls. Pin the vest to the front of the pincushion body so it covers the bottom edge of the ball. Wrap the vest around the sides of the ball and pin in place.

5 Pin the jacket over the vest. The sides and shoulders of the vest should be covered. Remove the jacket and reposition the vest if necessary. Glue or hand sew the vest and the jacket to the wool body ball, removing any pins as you work.

6 Glue the bow tie below the chin so the tips of the collar show above and the white "shirt" shows below.

7 Sew a flat flower button to the jacket lapel.

8 To make the top hat, sandwich the brim-base matboard ring between the hat-brim wool-blend felt pieces. Overcast the edges of the felt layers together with matching thread.

9 Butt the short ends of the hat-crown felt piece and overcast stitch them together to form a tube. Roll the crown cardboard into a tube and slide it into the wool crown. Let the cardboard unroll to fill the crown. Glue the wool to the cardboard at the hat seam.

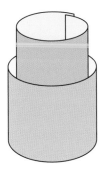

10 Overcast the hat-top piece to one end of the crown with matching thread. Push the top-base mat-board ring through the open end of the crown until it lays flat against the top of the hat.

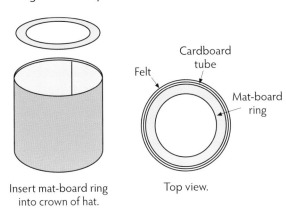

Felt
Cardboard tube
Mat-board ring

Insert mat-board ring into crown of hat.

Top view.

11 Lightly stuff the hat crown with roving or stuffing.

12 Pin the open end of the crown to the hat brim. With matching thread and a stab stitch (insert the needle down through the layers, and then back up through the layers in separate movements), stitch the lower edge of the crown wool to the brim wool, taking each stitch through both layers of the brim wool just inside the brim mat-board ring.

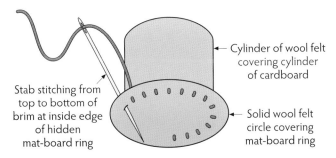

Stab stitching from top to bottom of brim at inside edge of hidden mat-board ring

Cylinder of wool felt covering cylinder of cardboard

Solid wool felt circle covering mat-board ring

13 Cut an X into the wool on the underside of the brim that spans the inside ring of the mat-board base. Avoid cutting any stitches.

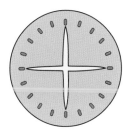

14 Push the flaps of wool to the inside of the hat and press the roving up to allow room for the top of Mr.'s head. Remove or add stuffing if necessary. Sew the hat to the head.

Make Mrs. Spoolkeep

1 Fold the bodice piece, right sides together, along the center line of one of the darts, matching the lower dots. Sew from the dot at the top of the dart to the matched dots at the bottom of the dart, securing the thread at both ends. Repeat to stitch the remaining darts on the top.

2 Sew the four pearl seed beads along one short edge of the bodice where indicated.

3 Sew the back seam of the skirt using a 1/8" seam allowance. Finger-press the seam allowance open.

4 Using a double strand of matching thread with the end knotted together, sew running stitches across the straight edge at the top of the skirt; do not cut the thread. Slide the skirt over the pincushion, with the front centered under the face. Pull the running stitches to gather the skirt tightly into the space between the spool and the body ball. Take several small stitches into the skirt to secure the gathers; cut the thread end.

5 Center and pin the bodice to the front of the body ball with the bottom edge tucked under the curve of the ball. Wrap the bodice around the ball, easing to fit. Lap the beaded edge over the non-beaded edge and hand sew the edges together with matching thread. Sew

the lower edge of the bodice to the body ball and tack the upper edge to the ball between each scallop.

6 Pinch the light-green bouquet scalloped circle around the shank of the flower button and stitch tightly through the shank loop to bunch the wool. Sew the wool scallopedcircle into the center of the green wool bouquet leaves. Tuck a flat flower button behind the edge of the wool scalloped circle and sew it to the leaves. Fold the ribbon strip in half crosswise and glue the layers together 1" from the fold. At the same spot, glue the bouquet to the ribbon. Glue the ribbon and bouquet to the lower bodice to the right of center.

7 String small pearl beads onto a length of white thread, filling 2½"; don't cut the thread. Wrap the bead string between the head and body ball and sew in place.

8 Knot a double strand of matching thread around a corner of the netting piece. Stitch through the holes of the netting along one long side, and then along the opposite side without cutting the thread. Pull the thread to gather the netting tightly; secure the thread ends. Glue the gathered netting to the head to the right of the top center. Choose a button large enough to cover the gathering thread and glue it in place.

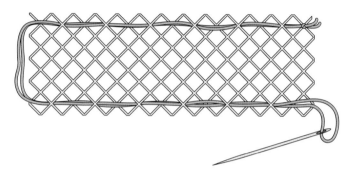

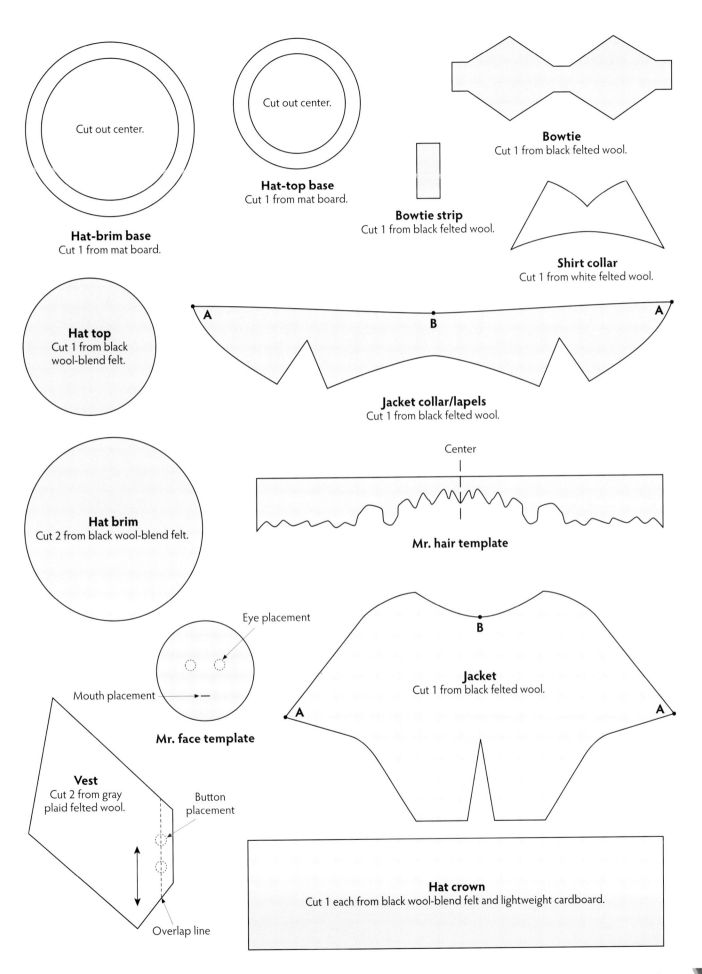

Hat-brim base
Cut 1 from mat board.

Cut out center.

Hat-top base
Cut 1 from mat board.

Cut out center.

Bowtie
Cut 1 from black felted wool.

Bowtie strip
Cut 1 from black felted wool.

Shirt collar
Cut 1 from white felted wool.

Hat top
Cut 1 from black wool-blend felt.

A   B   A

Jacket collar/lapels
Cut 1 from black felted wool.

Hat brim
Cut 2 from black wool-blend felt.

Center

Mr. hair template

Eye placement

Mouth placement

Mr. face template

Center: B

Jacket
Cut 1 from black felted wool.

A   A

Vest
Cut 2 from gray plaid felted wool.

Button placement

Overlap line

Hat crown
Cut 1 each from black wool-blend felt and lightweight cardboard.

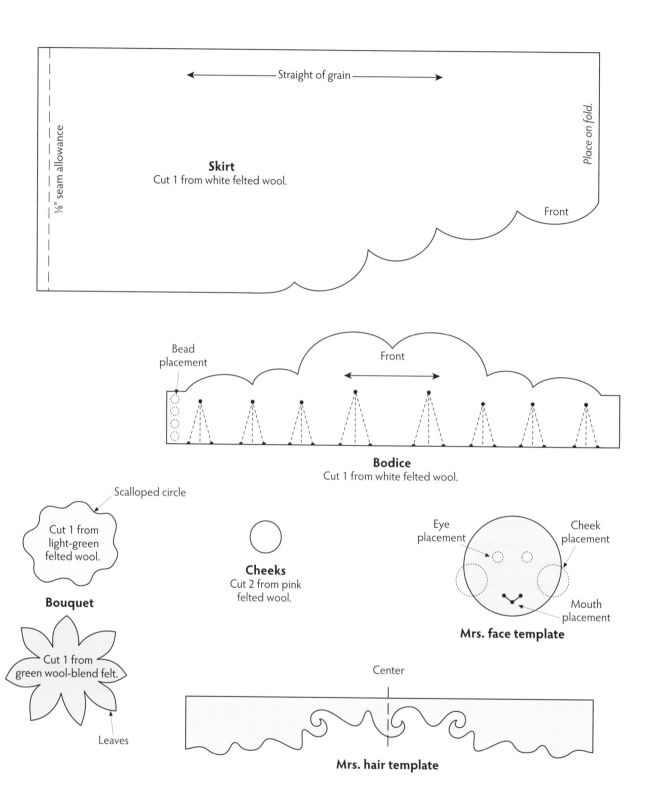

Skirt
Cut 1 from white felted wool.

Straight of grain

⅛" seam allowance

Place on fold.

Front

Bead placement

Front

Bodice
Cut 1 from white felted wool.

Scalloped circle

Cut 1 from light-green felted wool.

Bouquet

Cut 1 from green wool-blend felt.

Leaves

Cheeks
Cut 2 from pink felted wool.

Eye placement

Cheek placement

Mouth placement

Mrs. face template

Center

Mrs. hair template

A lthough the "Succulent Garden" pincushion looks complex, each element is rather simple to make. Use a variety of green wools to create visual interest.

Finished size: 5" x 6¾" x 5" (including pot)

Materials

5" x 12" piece of medium-green wool-blend felt for cactus

4" x 9" piece of blue-green felted wool for rosette

4" x 13" piece of yellow-green felted wool for rosette

4" x 9" piece of dark-olive wool-blend felt for jade plant

8" x 8" square of sage-green felted wool for sedum and flowerpot-base cover

1" x 17" strip of light-olive felted wool for draping succulents

½" x 10" strip of rose felted wool for draping succulents

2" x 11" piece of light-yellow cotton fabric, torn to create frayed edges, for cactus flower

6-strand embroidery floss: dark green

3" x 6" piece of mat board

Basic tools and supplies (page 6)

Terracotta flowerpot, 2½" tall x 3" diameter

Wool roving or polyester stuffing

Cutting

From the light-olive felted wool, cut:
  1 strip, ½" x 5"
  1 strip, ½" x 7"
  1 strip, ½" x 17"

From the sage-green felted wool, cut:
  5 strips, 1⅛" x 4¼"

Cut the Remaining Pieces

1 Use the patterns (pages 29 and 30) and refer to "General Instructions" (page 7) to make the patterns and cut out the pieces from the fabrics indicated. Mark the darts on the right side of each cactus-top piece. Mark the cutting line on each jade-plant strip.

2 Trace the cactus-bottom and flowerpot-base circles onto mat board and cut them out.

Make the Cactus

1 Fold each cactus top, wrong sides together, along the center line of the dart. Stitch from the dot at one end to the dot at the other end, following the pattern to stitch just outside the fold line.

2 Pin two cactus tops, wrong sides together, along one curved edge. Stitch from the top dot to the bottom dot. Repeat with the remaining two cactus-top pieces.

3 Open the two sets of cactus-top pieces and pin them wrong sides together. Sew from the top dot to the bottom dot along both curved edges, leaving the bottom edge open.

4 Stuff the cactus with wool roving or polyester stuffing, keeping the seams on the outside.

5 Using a double strand of matching thread with the ends knotted together, hand sew running stitches ⅛" from the lower edge of the cactus top; do not cut the thread. Push one of the mat-board base circles inside against the roving or stuffing and pull the stitches to close the opening.

6 Refer to "Making a Pincushion Base" (page 7) to gather the medium-green wool circle around the remaining mat-board base circle. Stitch it to the bottom of the cactus.

7 Hand stitch thorns on the cactus. Knot a single strand of the dark-green floss, leaving a ½" tail. Take a single stitch on a cactus seam and knot the thread close to the seam. Clip the thread, leaving a ½" tail. Randomly stitch three to five thorns on each seam.

Make the Rosette Succulent

1 Center the large top piece over the large bottom piece. With a running stitch and matching thread, sew the pieces together ⅛" from the edge of the top piece. Repeat with the medium and small rosette pieces.

2 Cut a ½" slit in the center of each of the bottom pieces. Loosely stuff a small piece of roving or stuffing inside each section of the leaves. Avoid stuffing the center area of each rosette.

3 Stack the leaf pieces largest to smallest with the dark sides down. Pin the rosette-center leaves to the top leaf in the stack in order from largest to smallest. Hand sew through the center of the stacked leaves several times, pulling the stitches snuggly so the center leaves fold up.

Make the Jade Plant

1 Cut the large and small jade-plant strips apart on the marked curved lines to make two pieces from each strip. Each curved piece of the strips is a leaf. With a double strand of matching thread with the ends knotted together, stitch a line of running stitches along the straight edge of each piece. Pull the stitches to gather the strip tightly.

2 Pinch the first leaf of a strip and twist it completely around twice to create a stalk. The wool will stay twisted. Twist the next leaf the same way, continuing until the entire strip is twisted. Repeat with each of the remaining strips.

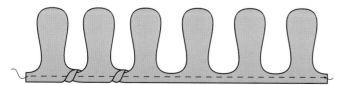

Knot the Draping Succulents

1 Tie five tight single knots along the length of the light-olive ½" x 7" strip. Stitch through the knots on both ends to keep them from loosening. Cut off the ends of the strip close to the knots. In the same manner, tie three knots in the light-olive ½" x 5" strip, stitch the knots, and cut off the strip ends.

2 Tie a knot at the end of the light-olive ½" x 17" strip. Lay the rose ½" x 10" strip on the light-olive strip with one end overlapping the knot. Tie a knot with both strips immediately above the light-olive knot. The knots should be touching.

3 Tie two knots close together in the green strip only. Bend those two knots out to the side and tie the next knot with the light-olive and rose strips.

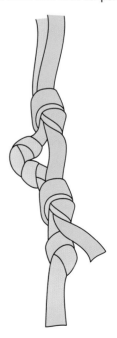

4 Tie a green knot only; then tie a knot with both strips; and then tie a green knot only.

5 Stitch through the knots at both ends of the strip and through the first and last knots that use the rose wool. Cut off the strip ends.

Make the Sedum

1 Fold a sage-green strip in thirds lengthwise. Tie a knot in the center of the folded strip and pull it tight. Hand sew through the knot to keep it tight, and then cut off the strip ends near the knot. Repeat with the remaining sage-green strips.

2 Fold a sedum leaf in half along the marked line, wrong sides together, but don't crease the fold. Using a double strand of matching thread with the ends knotted together, hand sew a running stitch ⅛" from the raw edges. Pull the thread to gather the leaf; knot the thread to secure the gathers and then cut the thread. Repeat with the remaining leaf shapes.

3 Arrange the leaves loosely around one knot at one end of each strip from step 1. Hand sew the leaves to the underside of the knot.

Make the Cactus Flower

1 Pull out several threads on both long edges of the cotton strip to create a frayed edge.

2 Fold the strip in half lengthwise, wrong sides together. Using a double strand of matching thread with the ends knotted together, sew a running stitch along the folded edge. Pull the thread to tightly gather the fabric. Tack the short edges of the strip together.

Assemble the Succulent Garden

1 Refer to "Making a Pincushion Base" to gather the sage-green wool around the flowerpot-base mat-board circle.

2 Place the covered base circle into the flowerpot with the gathered edge down and lightly mark a line on the inside of the flowerpot where it sits level. Remove the base and apply hot glue to the inside of the flowerpot just below the marked line. Place the base back into the flowerpot and press it into the glue. Allow the glue to cool.

3 Glue the base of the cactus to the flowerpot base ¼" from the edge of the flowerpot.

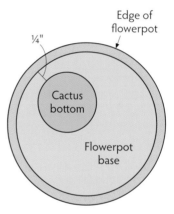

4 Turn the flowerpot with the cactus to the back. Pin all the remaining succulent elements in place, arranging them to fill the flowerpot. Glue each plant in place, removing the pins as you go.

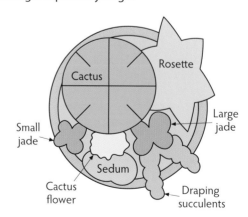

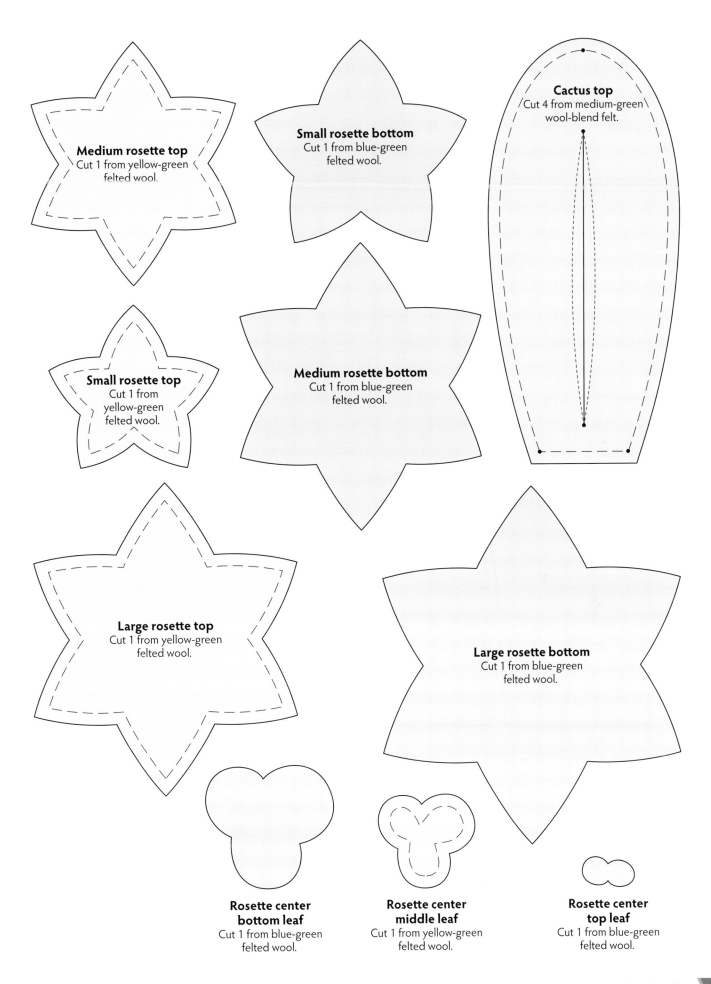

Medium rosette top
Cut 1 from yellow-green felted wool.

Small rosette bottom
Cut 1 from blue-green felted wool.

Cactus top
Cut 4 from medium-green wool-blend felt.

Small rosette top
Cut 1 from yellow-green felted wool.

Medium rosette bottom
Cut 1 from blue-green felted wool.

Large rosette top
Cut 1 from yellow-green felted wool.

Large rosette bottom
Cut 1 from blue-green felted wool.

Rosette center bottom leaf
Cut 1 from blue-green felted wool.

Rosette center middle leaf
Cut 1 from yellow-green felted wool.

Rosette center top leaf
Cut 1 from blue-green felted wool.

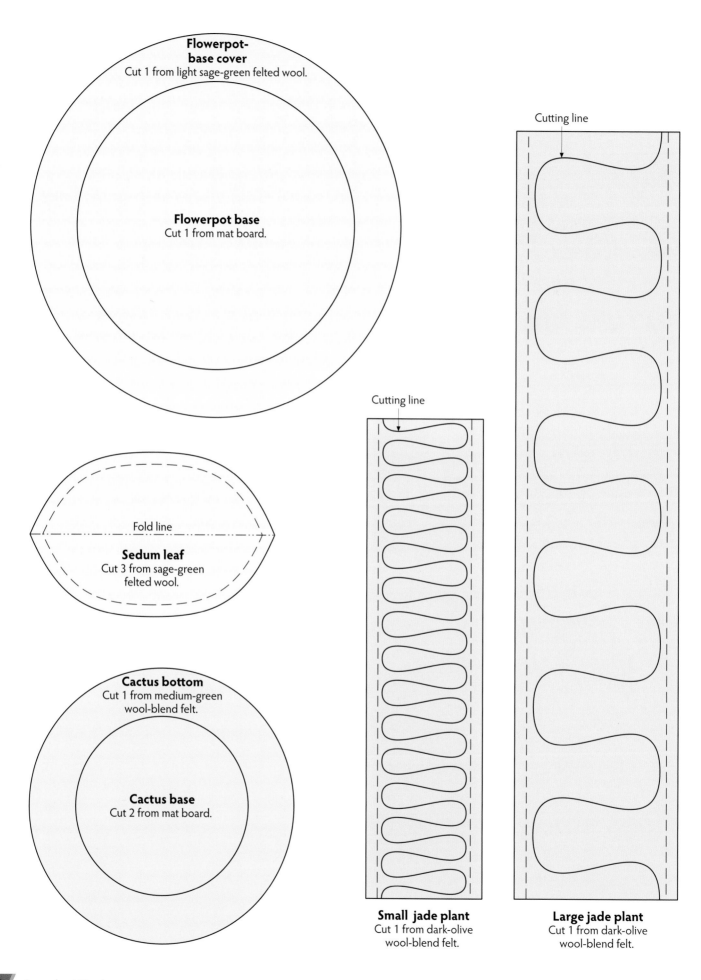

Flowerpot-base cover
Cut 1 from light sage-green felted wool.

Flowerpot base
Cut 1 from mat board.

Cutting line

Cutting line

Fold line

Sedum leaf
Cut 3 from sage-green
felted wool.

Cactus bottom
Cut 1 from medium-green
wool-blend felt.

Cactus base
Cut 2 from mat board.

Small jade plant
Cut 1 from dark-olive
wool-blend felt.

Large jade plant
Cut 1 from dark-olive
wool-blend felt.

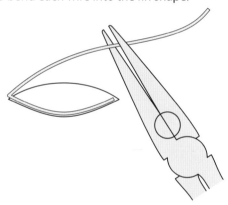

*F*loral wire is used creatively in this pincushion. It adds character when formed into water spouting from the whale, and when stitched inside the wool, it gives the fins and tail attitude.

Finished size: 6" x 4¾" x 4" (including spout)

Materials

10" x 10" square of aqua felted wool for whale

34" length of 20-gauge silver floral wire for spout and tail and fin shaping

Aqua pearl cotton, size 5, for mouth

Aqua two-hole ½"-diameter button for blowhole

2 black ¼"-diameter glass buttons for eyes

Wool roving or polyester stuffing

Basic tools and supplies (page 6)

Optional embellishments: Yellow and blue pins (from Just Another Button Company; see "Resources" on page 48)

Make the Whale Pieces

Hand or machine sew all seams using a ⅛" seam allowance, and secure the threads at the beginning and end of each seam.

1 Use the patterns (pages 33 and 34) and refer to "General Instructions" (page 7) to make the whale body, tail, and fin patterns and cut out the pieces from the aqua felted wool. Mark the dots and fold lines.

2 To make the body, fold the body piece in half on the fold line, right sides together with the A points aligned; pin around the outer edges. Sew from point A to point B along the curved edge.

3 Open the body and align points A and C.

4 Sew from point D to point E. Sew from point F to point G.

5 Turn the body right side out through the opening.

6 Stitch the aqua button to the top of the body where indicated for the blowhole.

7 Firmly stuff the body with wool roving or stuffing.

8 To make the fins, cut two 3½"-long pieces of wire. Follow the pattern (page 33) and use needle-nose pliers to bend each wire into the fin shape.

9 Fold each wool fin piece in half on the fold line, wrong sides together and sandwiching a wire fin between the wool layers. With a double strand of matching thread and a running stitch, stitch around each fin.

10 Cut a 10"-long piece of wire. Follow the pattern (page 34) to bend it into the tail shape. In the same manner as the fins, sandwich the wire tail between the two wool tail pieces and stitch around the edges.

Assemble the Whale

1 Slide the blunt end of the tail ½" into the opening at the base of the whale body, tucking the body seam allowance to the wrong side at the same time. Tack the tail to the seam allowance. Sew the opening closed with a ladder stitch (page 7).

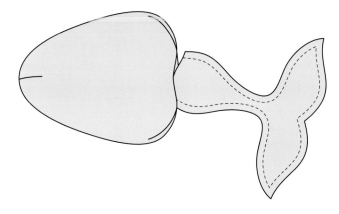

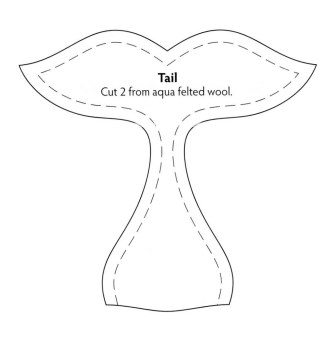

Tail
Cut 2 from aqua felted wool.

2 Tack the fins to the body at the marked points.

3 Sew a black button to each point marked for the eyes.

Fin wire shape
Make 2.

4 Stitch the mouth with pearl cotton. Make one long stitch from one marked point to the center front of the body, and then repeat on the other side.

5 Cut a 7"-long and a 10"-long piece of wire. Follow the patterns at right and use needle-nose pliers to bend the wires to form the water-spout shapes. Cut the straight end of each piece at an angle. Poke the two wire shapes through the holes on the aqua button and into the whale. Arrange the water spout shapes as desired; then carefully drop several drops of superglue in the two buttonholes and allow to dry.

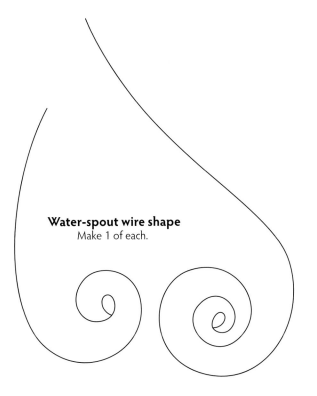

Water-spout wire shape
Make 1 of each.

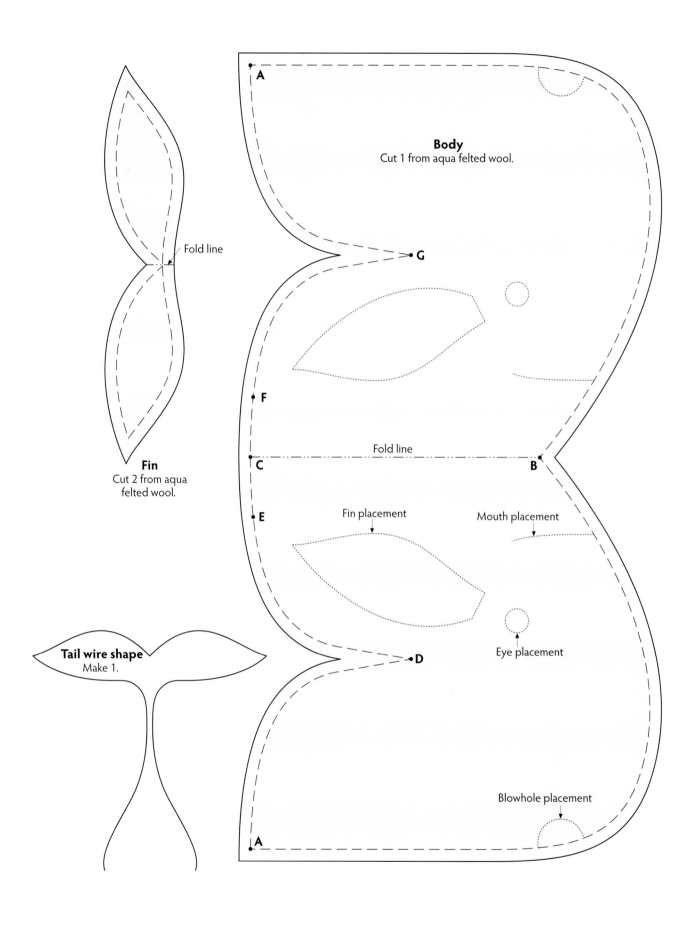

Fin
Cut 2 from aqua
felted wool.

Fold line

Body
Cut 1 from aqua felted wool.

A

G

F

Fold line

C

B

E

Fin placement

Mouth placement

Tail wire shape
Make 1.

D

Eye placement

A

Blowhole placement

The snowman, tree, and bird are each pincushions, and displayed together they have special appeal. Create a vignette built on a plate. Pose the pincushions and sprinkle old glass buttons around them for snow, and then top with a bell jar so you can enjoy your pincushion under glass.

Finished size: 2" x 5½" x 2" (snowman including bird on head)
3" x 6" x 3" (tree)
8" x 12" (bell jar)

Materials

11" x 17" piece of green felted wool for tree

8½" x 10" piece of white felted wool for snowman

2" x 10" piece of berry felted wool for large-bird wings and scarf

4 felted-wool balls: 3 cm white for snowman head, 1.5 cm bright pink for bird, 1 cm teal for bird, and 1 cm blue for bird

6-strand embroidery floss: teal, blue, black, and yellow

8 black seed beads for eyes

1 yellow ½"-diameter button for bird base

2 teal and 2 blue ¼"-diameter buttons for small-bird wings

Clear glass buttons in assorted sizes for "snow"

Round toothpick

2" x 2" square of mat board

Wooden skewer, 6"

2 wooden spools, 1¼" tall

White dinner plate with rim

Bell jar to fit inside rim of dinner plate, approximately 12" tall

Wool roving or polyester stuffing

Basic tools and supplies (page 6)

Optional embellishments: Mitten pins for snowman arms (from Just Another Button Company; see "Resources" on page 48)

Cutting

From the green felted wool, cut:
9 strips, 1" x 17"

From the berry felted wool, cut:
1 strip, ¾" x 10"
1 rectangle, 1" x 2"

Cut the Remaining Pieces

1 Use the patterns (pages 39) and refer to "General Instructions" (page 7) to make the patterns and cut out the pieces from the fabrics indicated.

2 Trace the snowman- and tree-base circles onto mat board and cut them out.

Assemble the Snowman

1 Pin two of the middle snowball pieces right sides together along one curved edge and hand or machine sew between the dots. Open the pieces and pin another middle snowball piece to one edge. Sew together between the dots. Add two more pieces in the same manner. Pin the edges of the first and last pieces together; sew, leaving a 1" opening.

2 Turn the snowball to the right side through the opening and stuff firmly with wool roving or polyester stuffing. Hand sew the opening closed with a ladder stitch (page 7).

3 Repeat step 1 for the bottom snowball, but do not leave an additional opening when sewing the first and last pieces together. You'll have an opening at the bottom of the piece. Fold the loose ends of the snowball pieces to the inside. Stuff firmly with roving or stuffing.

4 Push a mat-board circle against the roving or stuffing. Using matching thread, sew a running stitch along the opening edge; pull the thread to close the opening, and then secure the stitches.

5 Refer to "Making a Pincushion Base" (page 7) to gather the white wool circle around the remaining mat-board circle; stitch it to the bottom snowball.

6 Anchor a double strand of thread to the top center of the bottom snowball. Sew up through the center of the middle snowball through the points where the seams meet. Sew into the white felted-wool ball about 1" and bring the needle back out. Sew down through the middle snowball and take a small stitch at the top of the bottom snowball. Pull the thread snuggly to join the balls, and then secure the thread.

Embellish the Snowman

1 Tie a single knot in the berry ¾" x 10" strip, leaving 2" of wool extended beyond the knot, for the scarf. Hand sew a running stitch across the width of the scarf 2" from the other end of the scarf and pull the stitches to gather. Wrap the scarf around the snowman's neck, crossing the knot over the gathers, and sew it in place.

2 Use three strands of black floss to make four French knots (page 7) on the top snowball for the mouth, referring to the photo as necessary for placement.

3 Color the tip of the toothpick with an orange marker. Push the toothpick into the top snowball above the mouth until it's protruding from the front ⅜". Use wire cutters to cut off any toothpick that protrudes from the back of the snowball.

4 Sew two seed beads above the nose for the eyes.

5 Insert the mitten pins into the sides of the snowman for arms.

Make the Tree

1 Crosscut the green wool 1"-wide strips into the following lengths. Lay out the strips on your work surface in the order cut.

» 3 strips, 1" x 2½"
» 6 strips, 1" x 5½"
» 4 strips, 1" x 4"
» 5 strips, 1" x 5"
» 4 strips, 1" x 4"
» 3 strips, 1" x 3½"
» 3 strips, 1" x 3"
» 3 strips, 1" x 2½"
» 1 strip, 1" x 4½"

2 Using a hot-glue gun, glue one end of the wooden spool to the center of the mat-board circle. Fill the spool hole with hot glue and insert the wooden skewer with the pointed end up. Hold the skewer straight up while the glue cools.

3 Starting with the green 1" x 2½" strip, twist the strip once. Fold the strip in half so the ends meet. Push the ends opposite the fold over the skewer and down to the spool. Continue in this manner with all but the last strip, working in the order listed in step 1 and turning the tree as you add each strip.

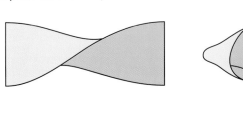

4 Fold one end of the final strip onto itself, leaving 1½" extended beyond the fold. Push the strip on the skewer through the two folded layers.

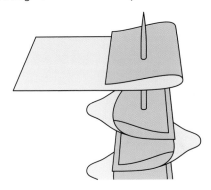

5 Fold the extended end in half lengthwise and put a drop of glue between the layers near the end, creating a pocket. Hot glue the pocket over the end of the skewer.

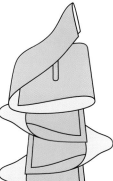

6 Arrange the wool pieces to evenly fill the tree.

Make the Birds

1 To make the large sitting bird, sew the yellow button to the bright-pink wool ball. Pinch one end of the ball to make a slight indentation for the bird's eyes. Using a size 10 Sharp needle and black thread, take a couple of stitches at one of the flattened areas. Place a bead on the needle and stitch through the head, with the needle coming out at the point for the second eye. Place a second bead on the needle and stitch back through the head. Pass through the first bead again, and then back through to the second bead, pulling the thread snugly so the eyes indent into the head a little. Secure the thread.

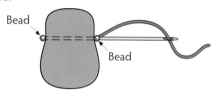

2 At the front of the bird, just below the eyes, make a ⅛"-long straight stitch with two strands of yellow floss to make the beak. Satin stitch (page 7) over the straight stitch to cover it.

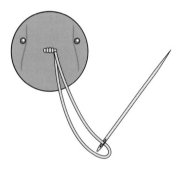

3 Sew a wing to each lower side of the bird.

4 Glue the two tail pieces together. Pin the tail to the back of the bird. Set the button side of the bird on the remaining wooden spool and make sure it sits evenly. Adjust the tail placement if necessary. Sew or glue the tail to the bird, and then glue the button side of the bird to the top of the spool.

5 To make the small birds that are pinned to the snowman's head and shoulder, refer to steps 1 and 2 to sew seed beads to the teal and blue felted-wool balls for the eyes and embroider the beak

6 Sew matching ¼" buttons to the sides of the balls for the wings.

7 Wrap a length of blue six-strand embroidery floss around a pencil five times. Thread the end of the floss through a needle and insert the needle under the wraps. Pull the floss end tight and then insert the needle under the wraps again and knot to secure the loops. Slide the loops off the pencil. Repeat with the teal floss.

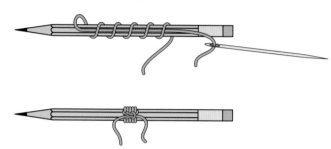

8 Sew the blue loops to the back of the blue bird for a tail. Cut the loops and fan out the floss. Trim the tail to about ⅜". Repeat with the teal loops on the teal bird.

9 Push a pin through each bird to attach it to the snowman.

Assemble the Snow Globe

Refer to the photo (page 35) to arrange the pincushions on the plate. Scatter the glass buttons on the plate around the pincushions, and then cover the scene with the bell jar.

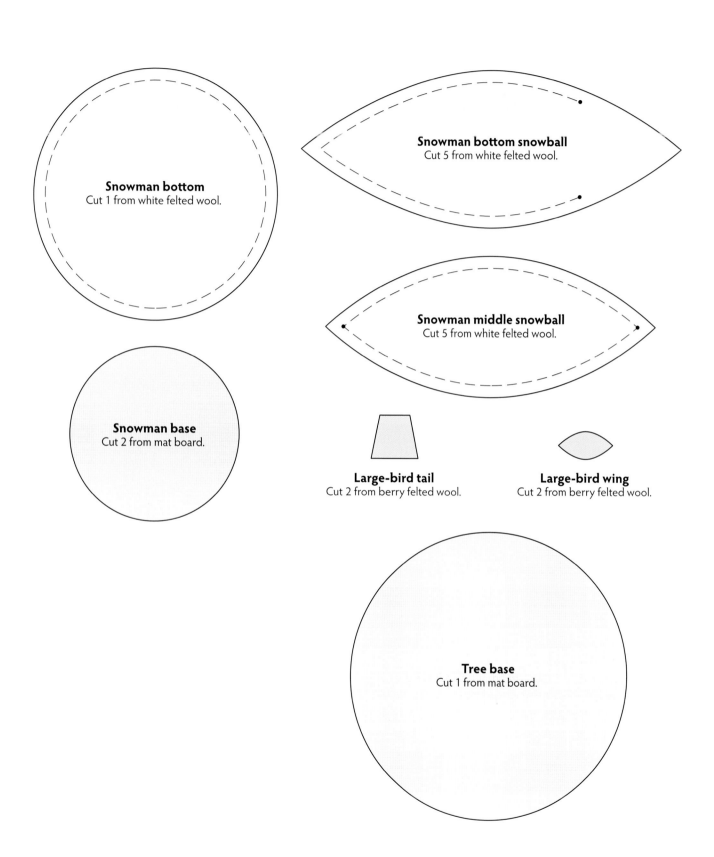

Snowman bottom
Cut 1 from white felted wool.

Snowman bottom snowball
Cut 5 from white felted wool.

Snowman middle snowball
Cut 5 from white felted wool.

Snowman base
Cut 2 from mat board.

Large-bird tail
Cut 2 from berry felted wool.

Large-bird wing
Cut 2 from berry felted wool.

Tree base
Cut 1 from mat board.

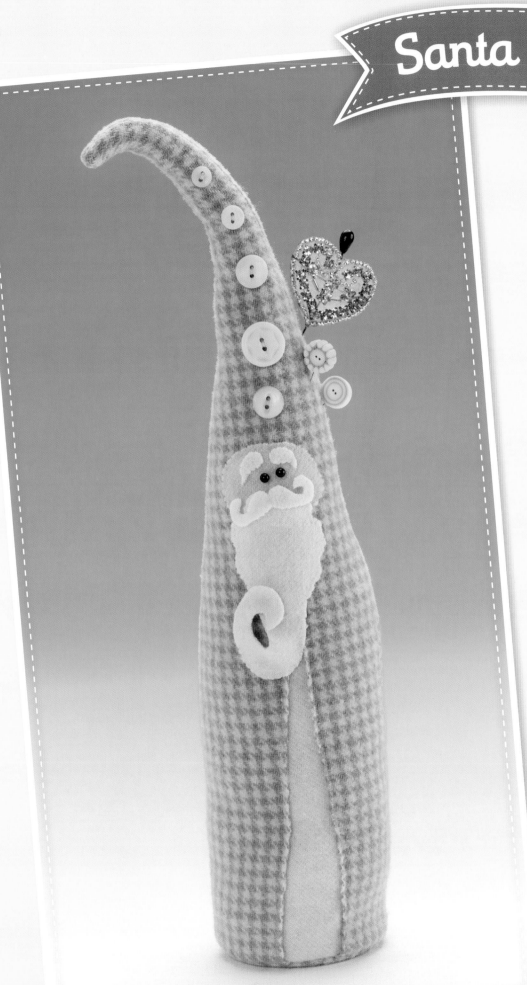

Large-scale pincushions like this Santa are ideal for displaying spectacular pins. Create your own pins using treasured vintage items from your stash. Affix special pieces to old hat pins or long corsage pins to create one-of-a-kind pincushion appeal.

Finished size: 3½" x 14" x 3½"

Materials

15" x 17" piece of aqua houndstooth felted wool for body

4½" x 7½" piece of cream felted wool for body gusset

2⅜" x 2⅞" piece of pink felted wool for face

5" x 5" square of white felted wool for eyebrows, mustache, and beard

3" x 6" piece of mat board

18" length of floral wire, 20 gauge

2 black 4 mm beads for eyes

5 assorted vintage buttons, ¼" to ¾" diameter

Wool roving or polyester stuffing

Optional embellishments: Vintage-inspired pins (from Just Another Button Company; see "Resources" on page 48)

Cut the Pieces

1 Use the patterns (pages 43 and 44) and refer to "General Instructions" (page 7) to make the patterns and cut out the pieces from the fabrics indicated. Transfer the gusset placement lines to the body piece.

2 Trace the Santa base onto mat board and cut it out.

Assemble the Body

1 Pin the cream gusset piece onto one of the body pieces where indicated, with the right side of the gusset against the wrong side of the body. Hand or machine sew through both layers along the two long sides and across the top of the gusset.

2 With the body side up, slide the scissors between the body and gusset layers. Holding the scissors flat against the aqua wool, trim ⅛" inside the line of stitching to reveal the gusset.

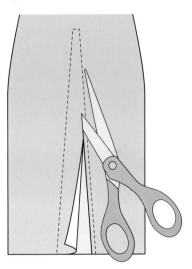

3 Pin the two body pieces right sides together. Sew along the sides and across the top point, leaving the bottom open.

4 Bend the wire into a V shape and place it on the seam line of the body back. Hand sew the wire to the seams. Turn the body right side out.

5 Fold up the bottom edge to the inside along the fold line and baste it in place. Firmly stuff the body with wool roving or polyester stuffing.

6 Refer to "Making a Pincushion Base" (page 7) to gather the aqua houndstooth circle around the mat-board circle; stitch it to the bottom of the Santa. Remove the bottom-edge basting stitches.

Finish

1 Pin the face piece to the body front where indicated on the pattern. Hand sew the face in place with a single strand of matching thread and an overcast stitch.

2 Pin the beard over the face where indicated on the pattern and overcast stitch it in place, curling the end of the beard onto the middle of the beard as shown and tacking it in place.

3 Pin the mustache over the top of the beard where indicated on the pattern. Tack it down with a few small stitches in the center of the mustache.

4 Overcast stitch the eyebrows in place.

5 Sew the black beads to the face for the eyes.

6 Bend the top of the body into a curve.

7 Sew a row of five mismatched buttons to the top of the Santa. Insert the vintage-inspired pins into the top of the Santa, referring to the photo on page 40 as needed.

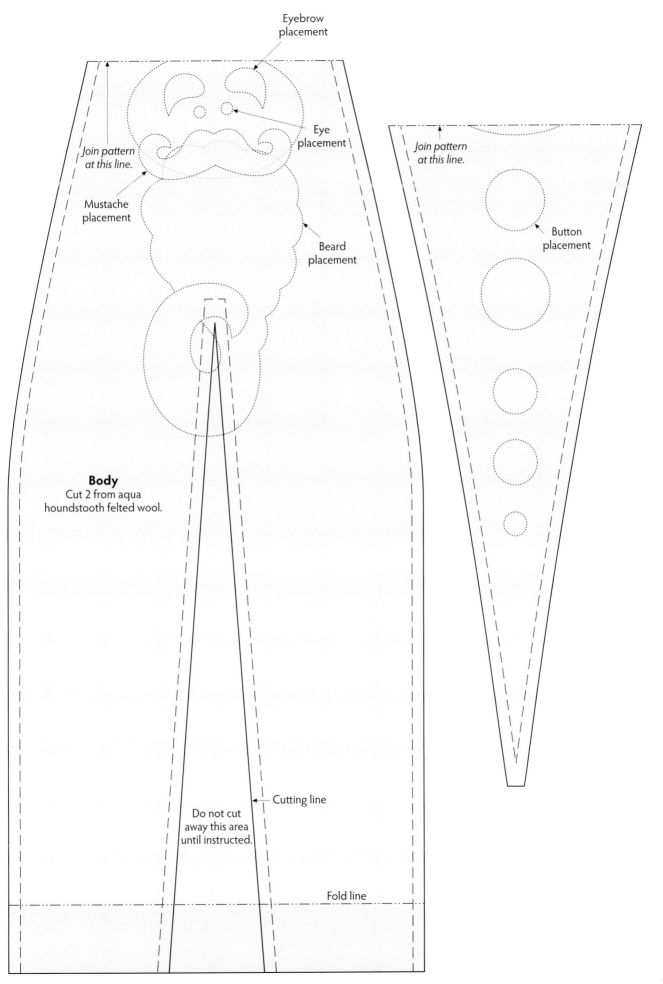

Eyebrow
placement

Eye
placement

*Join pattern
at this line.*

Mustache
placement

Beard
placement

Body
Cut 2 from aqua
houndstooth felted wool.

Cutting line

Do not cut
away this area
until instructed.

Fold line

*Join pattern
at this line.*

Button
placement

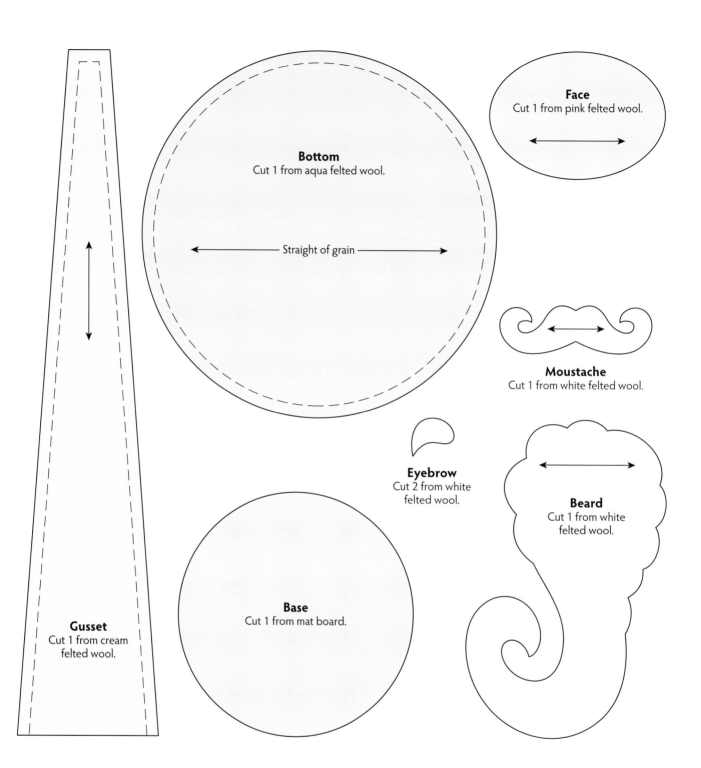

Face
Cut 1 from pink felted wool.

Bottom
Cut 1 from aqua felted wool.

Straight of grain

Moustache
Cut 1 from white felted wool.

Eyebrow
Cut 2 from white felted wool.

Beard
Cut 1 from white felted wool.

Gusset
Cut 1 from cream felted wool.

Base
Cut 1 from mat board.

*T*he traditional romantic lovebird image is updated by a collage of polymer-clay embellishments and dimensional wool flowers. Wool, pins, flowers, hearts, and birds—they're all together on this "love-ly" pincushion.

Finished size: 8" x 7⅞" x 3½"

Materials

8½" x 8½" square of white houndstooth felted wool for pillow front

8½" x 8½" piece of white felted wool for pillow back

6⅜" x 6¾" piece of deep-rose felted wool for heart

3¼" x 4½" piece of aqua felted wool for birds

2¼" x 3" piece of green herringbone felted wool for leaves

6" x 8" piece of deep-rose houndstooth felted wool for flowers

6-strand embroidery floss: deep rose and aqua

Wool roving or polyester stuffing

2 aqua-striped heart buttons for bird wings (from Just Another Button Company; see "Resources" on page 48)

Optional embellishments: Love pins (from Just Another Button Company; see "Resources")

Cut the Pieces

Use the patterns (page 47) and refer to "General Instructions" (page 7) to make the patterns and cut out the pieces from the fabrics indicated.

Appliqué the Pincushion Front

1 Pin the heart to the center of the white houndstooth square. Hand or machine appliqué the heart in place with a blanket stitch (page 7) and two strands of deep-rose floss.

2 Using two strands of aqua embroidery floss and a blanket stitch, appliqué the large bird to the heart using the placement guide; then add the small bird.

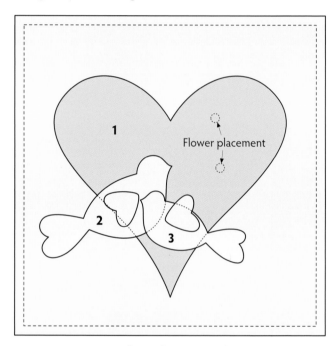

Appliqué placement guide

Finish and Embellish

1 Pin the pincushion top to the white wool square, right sides together. Stitch ¼" from the edges, leaving an opening along the bottom edge for turning. Turn the pincushion right side out through the opening.

2 Sew the aqua buttons to the birds for the wings.

3 Firmly stuff the pincushion with wool roving or polyester stuffing, and then sew the opening closed.

4 Using a double strand of matching thread with the ends knotted together, sew a running stitch ⅝" from the edges of a deep-rose houndstooth circle. Pull the thread to gather the circle into a ruffled blossom shape. Repeat with the remaining circles.

5 Pinch together the bases of four blossoms so that the ruffled edges form a flower. Sew the bases together and tack to the upper-right part of the heart.

6 Repeat step 5 with six blossoms and sew to the heart above the small bird. Sew the remaining blossom in the center of this group with the ruffled edge up.

7 Using a double strand of matching threadwith the ends knotted together, sew a running stitch on the marked lines and pull the thread to gather the leaves slightly. Tack the leaves to the pillow near the blossoms, referring to the photo as needed.

8 Insert the L-O-V-E pins above the large bird.

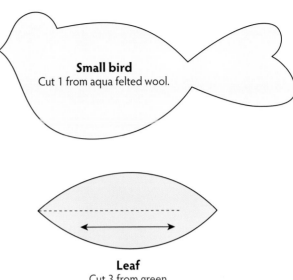

Small bird
Cut 1 from aqua felted wool.

Leaf
Cut 3 from green herringbone felted wool.

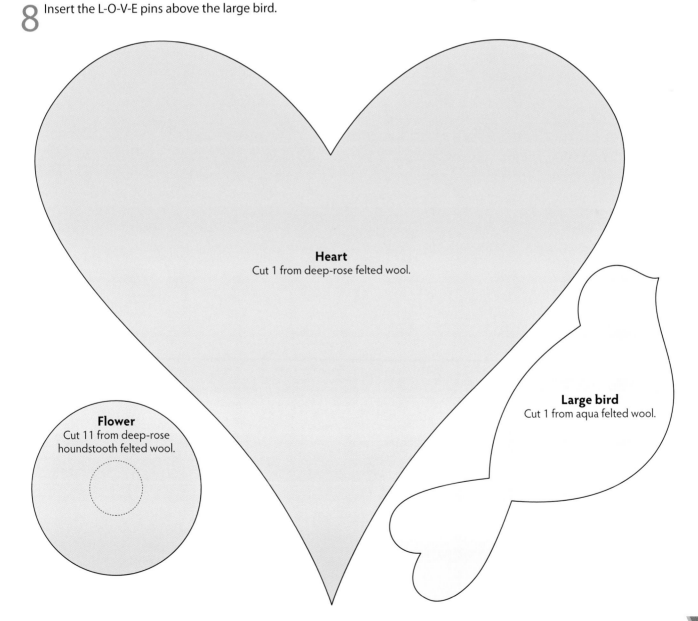

Heart
Cut 1 from deep-rose felted wool.

Flower
Cut 11 from deep-rose houndstooth felted wool.

Large bird
Cut 1 from aqua felted wool.

The mother and daughter team of Cecile and Rachel invite you to visit their website and blog. There you'll find their collections and creations—with special attention to pincushions, of course! Come share their mutual addiction to pincushions: www.ThePincushionEffect.com.

Cecile McPeak

Cecile McPeak learned to sew, craft, and "measure twice, cut once" from her creative parents, and she's proud to note that all three of her grown children are continuing the crafty family tradition. Part of the pleasure of her brand of creating is arranging a collection of inspiring materials—everything from old wooden spools and buttons to found objects, shells, stones, and sea glass. Someday these things might become part of a project, but in the meantime, they inspire creative thought.

Cecile feels fortunate to be part of the needle-arts industry as Founder and Creative Director of Just Another Button Company, a manufacturer of handmade polymer-clay buttons and pins. The buttons first appeared as ladybugs and bees on Cecile's silk-ribbon embroidery, and then gained popularity as whimsical embellishments by being featured in cross-stitching and quilting books from popular designers. Now Cecile leads the JABC design team in creating new buttons plus cross-stitch designs, quilt patterns, and dozens of pincushion kits and patterns.

Rachel Martin

Rachel Martin continues the family tradition of turning creative ideas into art. Her paper art has been presented through 2 Martins in a Nest, a company created in partnership with her husband, Joshua Martin. The company debuted in *Where Women Create* magazine, in an article featuring the Martins' handmade wedding.

Rachel is in the process of furnishing and decorating her turn-of-the-century St. Louis home in her own style—a mix of vintage collectibles and whimsical art. She works as a designer for Just Another Button Company, producing distinctive images for its product lines. She enjoys combining vintage images with fresh, modern colors.

Resources

Just Another Button Company
www.JustAnotherButtonCompany.com
Handmade buttons and decorative pins. Also available: embellishment kits for each project in this book, which include the pins and buttons made by Just Another Button Company.

Weeks Dye Works
www.WeeksDyeWorks.com
Hand-dyed woven felted wool and thread

HandBEHG Felts
www.HandBEHG.com
Felted-wool balls

Hillcreek Designs
www.HillCreekDesigns.com
Hand-dyed buttons

National Nonwovens
www.NationalNonwovens.com
WoolFelt (nonwoven wool-blend felt)